C000062037

A CATECHISM
for the use of
the people called
METHODISTS

Adopted by the Methodist Conference: 1986
Revised on the authority of the Conference: 2000

Revised with the insertion of hymns from Singing the Faith: 2013

FOREWORD

In its underlying aims, this Catechism follows its predecessor approved by the Methodist Conference of 1952. It sets out to provide as clear a statement as possible of the Christian faith. It is intended to be used with young people and adults. It is offered as a suitable tool for use in the preparation of Church members.

In the presentation, however, there are major differences, to take account of the changed context in which this Catechism will be used. The sections of the Catechism have been arranged to match, as far as possible, the experience of many of those coming into Church membership today. The Catechism begins with commitment to Jesus Christ. It continues with sections on the Christian life. It moves on to the Church and its beliefs, and concludes with a section on Methodism and the duties of Membership.

It has also been noted that many young people and adults coming into our churches are not familiar with traditional Christian language, or with the older versions of the Bible. All biblical references and quotations, therefore, are in The New Revised Standard Version, and a modern version of The Lord's Prayer is used. Theological terms are translated or explained.

To make the Catechism easier to use, cross references, biblical references, notes and references to Methodist documents are placed alongside the appropriate questions, rather than at the end of each section. This commentary material also includes suggestions for further study.

The Catechism is intended for use in groups studying with a leader. It is impossible in a short document, even with the addition of explanatory notes, to provide all the information that users will need. Groups taking the Catechism as the basis of their study are therefore encouraged to range outside the limits of the questions posed here. For the benefit of groups using the Catechism, a short act of worship is suggested at the end of each section.

It is not suggested that the answers in this Catechism, any more than those in the Catechism of 1952, should be learned by heart. What is stressed is the importance of using the Catechism alongside the Bible, so that the answers can be seen and understood against their biblical background.

Users of this Catechism are reminded that this is not the only approach to expressing, understanding and teaching the Christian faith. As has been stated above, this is 'a tool', provided to meet the needs of those who find this particular approach helpful. It is not envisaged that everyone seeking to explore the Christian faith will come this way.

Moreover, the use of this or any other tool is not an end in itself. It is only the beginning of, or a stage upon, a life-long process of learning, for it is into this that we are called when we are called into discipleship of Jesus Christ.

(a) WHAT IS A CHRISTIAN?

1. **What is a Christian?**
   Christians are those who believe that God has revealed himself in Jesus Christ, accept Jesus Christ as their Lord and Saviour, live in communion with God and in the power of the Holy Spirit, and take their place in the fellowship of Christ's Church.

2. **What is a Christian's calling?**
   A Christian is called by God to trust and follow Jesus Christ; to keep company with him; to learn from his words and actions; and to share in his mission, in the power of the Holy Spirit, in company with other Christians.

3. **What is the mission of Jesus Christ?**
   To proclaim the coming of God's kingdom, to call people to repent and to receive the kingdom of God, to turn from their sins and believe the Good News.

4. **What is repentance?**
   Repentance is turning in sorrow away from sin and turning to God to seek forgiveness and new life in Jesus Christ.

5. **What is sin?**
   Sin is the condition of estrangement from God which affects the whole human race. Sins are specific actions, words or thoughts which arise from our sinful condition and deny the presence, power and purpose of God.

1. God: see 56, 57

    Jesus Christ: 'Christ' comes from the Greek word *christos* which means 'anointed' and is a translation of the Hebrew word from which we get 'Messiah'. Jesus is called the Christ because he is the one chosen by God to fulfil his purposes, recorded in the Old Testament, the holy book of the Jewish nation. The Jews looked forward to a promised King who would serve God's people and establish a reign of peace for the whole human race.
    See also: 58, 59, 60, 61

    Holy Spirit: see 62   Communion with God: see 37
    Church: see 43

    Acts 11:26   John 1:1-5, 14-18
    John 14:8-11   Hebrews 1:1-3

2. Mark 1:16-20; 3:13-15
    John 20:21-22   Acts 1:8

3. Kingdom of God: see 22   Good News: see 7
    Repentance: see 4   Sin: see 5

    Mark 1:14-15

4. Luke 3:1-14; 15:17-20   Amos 5:10-15
    Psalm 51:1-14

5. Romans 3:9-18, 23; 7:13-20   Psalm 51:1-5

    Note: Various words are used in the Bible for sin, with different shades of meaning, for example: offence (against moral laws), injustice, failure, lawlessness, godlessness.

    Bible: see 52

6. **What are the effects of sin?**
Sin hinders the effects of God's grace. It corrupts our relationships with him and with one another, with the world in which we live and with ourselves. The effect of sin is discord, where God intended harmony.

7. **What is the Good News?**
That God has acted decisively in Jesus Christ to deal with our sinful condition: that is, he has acted to save us. God offers us his love, forgiveness, acceptance and new life in Christ.

8. **What is salvation?**
Salvation is the forgiveness of our sin, deliverance from guilt, and the gift of new life in Christ. It is a process that begins now, gives us victory over death and is completed with God in heaven.

(a) **Further study**
Methodist Worship Book, pages 97-102

(b) **WHAT DOES GOD DO FOR US IN CHRIST?**

9. **How does God save us?**
God, as a free gift, converts us by his grace, turning us from rebels into friends. He puts us right with himself, gives us new life in Christ, and makes us his own holy people through the Holy Spirit. We receive his gifts when we turn to him in repentance and put our faith in Jesus Christ who was crucified and raised again for us.

10. **What is grace?**
Grace is God's sovereign love and favour, freely given to undeserving and hostile people.

6. Grace: see 10

   Genesis 3:14-19   James 4:1-3

7. John 3:16   Acts 10:36-43

8. Heaven: see 18

   Mark 2:1-4; 10:28-31, 45
   2 Corinthians 5:18-21   Romans 5:15-21

(a) **Worship**
    Reading: John 1:35-41
    Hymn: *Singing the Faith* 556
    Prayer: *Methodist Worship Book*, page 529,
                 fourth prayer

9. Conversion: see 11   Grace: see 10
   Holy Spirit: see 62   Repentance: see 4
   Faith: see 12

   Mark 1:14-20   Romans 5:1-11
   1 Peter 1:18-21; 2:10

10. Sovereign: because he gives his grace freely to all
    people, not according to human merit.

    John 3:16   Luke 15   Matthew 11:28-30
    Ephesians 2:4-9   Romans 5:6-8

11. **What is conversion?**
It is the change which God works in us as we respond to his grace in repentance and faith.

12. **What is faith in Jesus Christ?**
Faith in Jesus Christ is trusting that through him alone God gives us his salvation. We demonstrate our faith by desiring to do God's will and by the practical love we show to others.

13. **What has Jesus done?**
Jesus Christ came to reveal God to men and women and to offer them God's grace. To achieve this he shared their human life and death, dying on the cross. God brought him back from death with great power and glory, thereby conquering death and sin, and opening the kingdom of God to all believers.

14. **How are we to understand Jesus Christ's death and resurrection?**
Jesus Christ suffered death and was raised again for us, so that we might live for him. The Bible uses various expressions for this, of which the following are a few examples:

- he gave his life to redeem all people;
- he is compared with the Passover Lamb, sacrificed as a sign of God's freeing of his people;
- he is also compared with the lamb sacrificed on the Day of Atonement;
- being joined to Christ is described as a new creation;
- by his death and resurrection Christ has defeated the powers of evil.

None of these is complete by itself: together they point to the fact that through the cross God acted decisively on behalf of the world he had created.

15. **What is the new birth?**
New birth, regeneration and conversion are all terms used to describe the process by which we are brought by God from the state of sin into the new life in Jesus Christ, in which we grow through the working of the Holy Spirit in us.

11. Acts 26:18; 9:1-21   Ephesians 4:22-24

Note: Paul's conversion should not be taken as a model for all conversions. For many people it is a more gradual process, with no dramatic turning point.

12. Ephesians 2:4-10   James 2:14-26
    Acts 16:29-31

13. Believers: those who have faith in him.

Jesus Christ's work: see 58, 59, 60, 61

Philippians 2:5-11   Romans 8:31-39
John 3:16   2 Corinthians 8:9

14. Jesus Christ's death: see 60

- the idea is of a ransom price paid to buy us for God:
  Mark 10:45   Isaiah 53
- the blood of the Passover Lamb, sprinkled on the doorposts of the houses of the Hebrews, protected them when the angel of death passed over Egypt, as a result of which the Egyptians set the Hebrews free: 1 Corinthians 6:7   Exodus 12
- the lamb was killed to atone for or cover the sins of the people: 1 John 2:2   Revelation 5
  Romans 5:6-11
- God's work of salvation is seen as a new creation:
  2 Corinthians 5:14-18
- the powers of evil are no longer able to hold in slavery those who believe in Jesus Christ:
  Colossians 2:11-15

15. John 3:1-8, 14-17   Ephesians 2:1-5

16. **How are we put right with God?**
    We are put right with God (that is, justified) when God
    forgives our sin, accepts us, declares us to be his
    children, and restores our relationship with himself, on
    the basis of what Jesus Christ has done, to which we
    respond by faith in him.

17. **How do we become God's holy people?**
    We become God's holy people (that is, we are
    sanctified) through the work of the Holy Spirit in our
    lives. As we are renewed from within, we are
    transformed by God's patient love into the likeness of
    Christ, we are given the power to do the will of our
    Father, and we grow up into Christian maturity,
    individually and corporately.

18. **How can we be assured of our salvation?**
    Through the promises given us in the Bible, by the
    inner assurance given us by the Holy Spirit, by the
    evidence in our actions of God's working within us,
    and through the encouragement of fellow Christians.

19. **What is the state of those who refuse to repent and
    turn to God?**
    They continue to be under the judgement of God and
    to be separated from him.

20. **What is the promise of God to those who persevere
    in faith to their lives' end?**
    The abundant life which they have already begun to
    enjoy will become theirs in full measure, they will
    experience for themselves Christ's victory over death,
    and they will share fully the eternal joy of all believers
    in the presence of God. That is what is meant by
    heaven.

(b) **Further study**
    John Wesley's account of his spiritual pilgrimage
    (*Journal* for 24 May 1738) or some other short
    Christian biography or autobiography (recognising
    that the experience of one Christian will be different
    from that of others).

16. Forgiveness: see 63
    1 Corinthians 1:26-31   Romans 8:1
    See also the passages referred to above in 13 and 14.

17. 1 Peter 2:9-10   Romans 12:1-21
    Ephesians 3:14-21; 4:12-16

    Note: 'Holy', as applied to people and things, means
    first of all 'set apart for God's exclusive use'. As
    applied to God, it refers to that which makes him God,
    wholly different from human beings, awe-inspiring,
    glorious, yet not separated by distance so much as by
    nature.

18. Romans 8:14-17, 31-39   Hebrews 10:23-25
    2 Timothy 2:11-13   Galatians 5:19-23
    1 John 1:5-2:6   John 10:27-30

    Note: The Bible does not encourage us to rely on our
    feelings alone.

19. Judgement: see 61

    Matthew 7:13-14, 21-27   John 3:18
    Matthew 25:31-46

20. Christian hope: see 64

    Luke 23:40-43
    John 10:10; 11:25-26; 6:40
    1 Corinthians 13:8-13; 15:12-57

(b) **Worship**
    Reading: Romans 8:1-17
    Hymn: *Singing the Faith* 357
    Prayer: *Methodist Worship Book*, page 540,
                  second prayer

(c) THE CHRISTIAN LIFE: NEW LIFE IN ACTION

21. What is the new life?

It is the life in the power of the Holy Spirit which is lived by those whom God has made heirs of his kingdom through the saving work of Christ.

22. What is the kingdom of God?

It is his rightful reign over everything he has made, at present fully recognised only by those who have accepted it in Jesus Christ. In the end, God's rule will be acknowledged by all and established undisputed when he judges the whole human race through Jesus Christ.

23. How can we obey God's rule?

We do everything out of thankfulness for his love for us, shown above all in Jesus Christ. We do God's will by the power of the Holy Spirit whom he gives us.

24. How does God guide us?

God guides us from within, through the Holy Spirit's prompting of our conscience. He guides us through the Bible, as we study its teaching. He guides us through Christian fellowship, the advice of friends, and as we respond to daily events and circumstances. He guides us particularly as we seek to be imitators of Jesus Christ.

25. Where do we find the way God wants us to live?

God's purpose for us is that his law should be written in our wills, so that our motive for action comes from within. One effect of our sin, however, is that we are, at best, only imperfectly aware of God's law within. So God has given us his law in other ways.

In summary form it is found in the commandments of the Old and New Testaments. It is developed and applied in the life and teaching of Jesus. It is the work of the Holy Spirit to write it afresh in the hearts of God's people.

21. Kingdom: see 22

Romans 8:1-17

22. 1 Corinthians 15:24-28   Revelation 4:11
Mark 1:14-15   Matthew 13:24-33

23. John 15:5-7   Colossians 3:17
Romans 8:1-11

24. John 16:12-15   Acts 16:6-10
1 Timothy 5:23

Note: This answer is not intended to imply that discovering God's guidance is easy. Our consciences, our understanding of the Bible, our prayers, even the advice of our friends, may be coloured by prejudice, social custom or political ideology.

25. Old and New Testaments: see 52

Law: The word means something nearer to instruction than our modern word law.

Jeremiah 31:31-34   Exodus 20: 1-17
Matthew 5:13-6:34

26. What are the Ten Commandments?

Prologue: I am the Lord your God, who brought you out of the land of Egypt, out of the house of slavery.

1. You shall have no other gods before me..

2. You shall not make for yourself an idol, whether in the form of anything that is in heaven above, or that is on the earth beneath, or that is in the water under the earth. You shall not bow down to them or worship them, for I the Lord your God am a jealous God, punishing children for the iniquity of parents, to the third and fourth generation of those who reject me, but showing my steadfast love to the thousandth generation of those who love me and keep my commandments.

3. You shall not make wrongful use of the name of the Lord your God, for the Lord will not acquit anyone who misuses his name.

4. Remember the sabbath day and keep it holy. For six days you shall labour and do all your work. But the seventh day is a sabbath to the Lord your God; you shall not do any work – you, your son or daughter, your male or female slave, your livestock, or the alien resident in your towns. For in six days the Lord made heaven and earth, the sea, and all that is in them, but rested the seventh day; therefore the Lord blessed the sabbath day and consecrated it.

5. Honour your father and your mother, so that your days may be long in the land that the Lord your God is giving you.

6. You shall not murder.

7. You shall not commit adultery.

8. You shall not steal.

9. You shall not bear false witness against your neighbour.

10. You shall not covet your neighbour's house; you shall not covet your neighbour's wife, or male or female slave, or ox, or donkey, or anything that belongs to your neighbour.

26. Prologue: Note that the Ten Commandments (Exodus 20:1-17) are a response to what God has done, not a formula for winning his favour.

Each Commandment should be studied alongside the teaching of Christ and the apostles (referred to below) which interprets it.

1. John 4:22-24   Matthew 6:33
   1 Corinthians 8:5-6

2. Acts 17:16-31   Galatians 4:1-10

3. Matthew 5:33-37

4. Mark 2:23-3:6   Acts 16:7

5. Mark 7:9-13   Ephesians 6:1-4

6. Matthew 5:21-24   Romans 12:17-21

7. Matthew 5:27-30   1 Corinthians 6:12-20

8. Ephesians 4:28

9. Ephesians 4:25, 29-32

10. James 4:1-10

27. **What does God teach us in the Ten Commandments?**
He teaches us how to respond to his grace by loving and worshipping him and loving our neighbour.

28. **How did Jesus interpret the Ten Commandments?**
He applied them, not only to our outward actions but to our inward thoughts and intentions, by revealing their full demands; he condemned unrighteous anger, lust and hatred, pride and anxiety. He also taught that faith in God means more than obeying commandments; it is giving our whole selves in trust to him.

29. **How did Jesus sum up the Commandments?**
He said: 'Love the Lord your God with all your heart, with all your soul, and with all your mind.' This is the greatest and the most important commandment. The second most important commandment is like it: 'Love your neighbour as you love yourself.' He also said: 'And now I give you a new commandment: love one another. As I have loved you, so you must love one another.'

30. **How do we show our love to God?**
We show our love to God when we worship and serve him with joy, faith and obedience.

31. **How do we love our neighbour as ourselves?**
We love our neighbour as ourselves by doing for our neighbour everything we would like others to do for us. Jesus showed what such love might mean by dying for others.

32. **Who is our neighbour?**
Our neighbour is whoever we meet, or to whom we can show love. There are no limits, of race, religion or geography, to those to whom we should show neighbourly love.

33. **How is God's law fulfilled?**
God's law reveals his will. Jesus Christ fulfilled, in perfect love, his Father's will. He gives us power to do the same by his example and by his inward presence through the Holy Spirit.

27. Worship: see 46

    Deuteronomy 6:5   Leviticus 19:18

28. Faith in God: see 56

    See the references to the teaching of Jesus above, also
    Matthew 19:16-22

29. Neighbour: see 30

    Deuteronomy 6:5   Leviticus 19:18
    Matthew 22:34-40   John 13:1-17,
                                     34; 15:11-17

30. 1 John 4:7-21
    John 14:21-24; 15:10

31. Matthew 7:12   1 John 3:11-18

32. Luke 10:25-37   James 2:14-17

33. Perfect love: see 35

    Romans 13:10   John 12:49-50; 13:10

34. **What are the marks of those who do the will of God?**
They show the fruit of the Spirit: love, joy, peace, patience, kindness, goodness, faithfulness, gentleness and self-control. But the greatest gift is love.

35. **What is Christian perfection?**
Through the Holy Spirit God has given us his love so that we may love him in return with all our heart, soul, mind and strength, and our neighbour as ourselves. This gift is offered to all Christians, and by responding we affirm that there is no limit to what the grace of God is able to do in a human life. By giving us the Holy Spirit, God assures us of his love for us and enables us to love as he, in Christ, loves us. When God's love is perfected in us, we so represent Christ to our neighbours that they see him in us without hindrance from us.

Perfect love, as Christian perfection is also called, is the result of, and can only be maintained by, complete dependence on Jesus Christ. It is given either gradually or at one moment, but does not mean that spiritual growth has ended, for Christian perfection is perfection in love only: it is not freedom from making mistakes, or from ignorance. Only God is absolutely perfect.

(c) **Further study**
The new life has social implications, as well as demanding a new life-style of the individual. Our new life will affect our attitudes to such issues as the use of natural resources, money and power; peace, war and justice; the plight of the poor, the weak and the helpless. Begin a study of these issues from Isaiah 1-10, Amos and Micah.

(d) THE CHRISTIAN LIFE: PRAYER

36. **What is prayer?**
Prayer is the communication, spoken and unspoken, that takes place between ourselves and God.

34. John 13:35   1 Corinthians 12:31-13:13
Galatians 5:22-26

35. Romans 8:12-17   1 John 4:7-21   Romans 5:5

Note: Christian perfection or perfect love was a particular emphasis in John Wesley's preaching and writing: see *A Plain Account of Christian Perfection* and the sermons on the subject based on Philippians 3:12 and Hebrews 6:1.

Wesley: see 66 and accompanying notes.

(c) Worship
Reading: John 15:16-27
Hymn: *Singing the Faith* 727
Prayer: *Methodist Worship Book*, page 549,
first prayer

36. Matthew 6:5-14   Romans 8:26-27

37. Why do we need to pray?

We need to pray because we were created for friendship with God and have been reconciled to him in Jesus Christ. Prayer is the natural expression of this loving relationship with God our heavenly Father. We pray to him because we trust him and want to do his will in everything. We pray to him because we depend on him and seek his guidance, strength and comfort. Jesus himself frequently prayed and taught his disciples to do likewise.

38. What should our prayers include?

Our prayers should include:

Adoration – we praise and worship God for what he is;

Confession – we come to God in penitence, admitting what we are and seeking his forgiveness;

Intercession – we pray to God on behalf of others;

Petition – we pray to God about our own needs and concerns;

Thanksgiving – we thank him for all that he has given us, especially for our salvation in Jesus Christ.

Meditation – we reflect quietly on the nature of God and what he has done, and wait for him to speak to us.

39. Does God always hear our prayers?

God always hears our prayers, but does not always answer immediately or in the way we expect. Or he may answer, and we fail to realise that he has done so. Or we may be the means by which God answers our own prayers or those of others.

40. How did Jesus teach us to pray?

He gave us the prayer we call The Lord's Prayer, which is both a prayer for us to use and a model for our own prayers.

37. Luke 11:1-13; 18:1-8; 22:39-46
    Romans 8:14-17   James 1:2-8

    Note: Prayer is the 'natural' expression of our
    relationship to God, but that does not mean that we
    necessarily find prayer easy. We have to learn to pray
    as a child has to learn to talk. God is aware of our
    difficulties, and gives us the help of the Holy Spirit.

    Note: Reconciled – Jesus Christ has broken down the
    barriers between us and God, restoring the relationship
    between us. 2 Corinthians 5:17-19

38. Psalm 18   Revelation 4:8; 15:3-4
    Psalm 51
    Psalm 72
    Psalm 6   Philippians 4:6
    Psalm 30   1 Thessalonians 1:2-3

    Worship: see 46

39. Matthew 6:7-8   James 4:1-10
    2 Corinthians 12:7-10
    2 Samuel 12:15-23

40. Jesus' teaching on prayer: see 37 (notes)

    Matthew 6:9-13

41. What is the Lord's Prayer?

Our Father in heaven,
hallowed be your Name,
your kingdom come,
your will be done,
on earth as in heaven.
Give us today our daily bread.
Forgive us our sins
as we forgive those who sin against us.
Save us from the time of trial
and deliver us from evil.
For the kingdom, the power,
and the glory are yours,
now and for ever. *Amen.*

42. Why do we pray in the name of Christ?

To pray in his name is to pray with his authority, as those whom he has saved and reconciled to God. To pray in his name implies, also, that what we are asking is what he himself would ask for us; that is, it is in accordance with his will, and that we submit our requests to that test.

(d) Further study

There are many books of prayer, classics from the past and the works of modern writers, which repay study. The Book of Psalms, the prayers of Jesus and the apostles in the New Testament, *Singing the Faith* and the *Methodist Worship Book* are all rich resources in which to discover more about prayer. Keep a notebook into which you copy prayers, from all sources, which you find particularly helpful.

41. Note: For the traditional, and alternative modern versions of the Lord's Prayer, see the *Methodist Worship Book* or *Singing the Faith*. The ending of the Lord's Prayer, 'For the kingdom, etc' was not in the original text of Matthew's Gospel, but was added later by the early Church.

42. John 14:11-14; 16:23-24
    James 4:1-10

(d) Worship
Reading: Luke 11:1-13
Hymn: *Singing the Faith* 519, 529
Prayer: *Methodist Worship Book*, page 342

(e) THE CHURCH AND THE CHURCHES

43. What is the Church?

The Church is all those on earth and in heaven who have been called by God, through Jesus Christ, to be his people, and who share the unity that the Spirit gives. The Spirit guides the Church, and equips its members with varied gifts, so that they may support one another, encourage one another and serve their neighbours with joy. The universal Church takes the form of local congregations, where the message of Christ received through the apostles is preached, where God is glorified in the celebration of the sacraments and other acts of worship, and Christians share the Christian life.

44. Who exercises the ministry of the Church?

Christ offered himself as a servant or minister and opened the way to God for us (his priestly ministry). All Christians are called to continue Christ's ministry by serving in the Church and in the world. By the Holy Spirit he equips them with spiritual gifts, for the benefit of the whole body in its disciplined life, and for its service to the whole world. As all members of the Church share the privilege and responsibility of direct access to God, all are called to bring others into personal relationship with him, and to pray for everyone. This is what we mean by 'the priesthood of all believers'.

45. How is the ministry of the Church exercised?

The ministry of the Church is exercised as Christians respond to God's call and discover and use the gifts which the Holy Spirit has given them. Some callings are matched by the Church's acts of appointment, when those whose vocations have been tested are commended to God's help. Among these are the ordained ministries of presbyters (ministers of the word and sacraments) and deacons. Whether or not their calling is recognised by some form of commissioning, all Christians share in the service to which the Church is called.

43. Church: see 63
    Sacraments: see 47, 48, 49

    Ephesians 4:1-6   1 Peter 2:9-10
    1 Thessalonians 1:1   Philemon 1:2
    1 Corinthians 14:26-32   Colossians 4:15-17

    On the disunity of the Church: see 50

44. Mark 10:43-45   Ephesians 4:7-16
    1 Corinthians 12:4-31   Romans 12:3-8
    1 Peter 2:9   John 13:12-17
    Hebrews 13:15-16

    Ministry, service: the words most frequently used in
    the New Testament are those used also of people who
    wait at table.

45. Romans 12:3-8   Acts 13:1-3
    1 Timothy 3:8-10; 4:14

    Note: The ordained ministries of presbyters and
    deacons are only two of the many ministries
    recognised by the Churches. Not all these ministries
    are recognised by ordination: for example, in the
    Methodist Church local preachers, workers with
    children and young people and pastoral visitors are
    recognised and commissioned in different ways.
    There are also administrative and practical ministries
    which often receive no formal recognition. Deed of
    Union, clause 4, Standing Order 600.

46. What is the worship of God?

To worship is joyfully to proclaim, in the power of the Spirit, the wonderful acts of God and to celebrate his glorious nature. We worship God, not only in formal or informal acts of worship, but also with our lives, by serving him in serving other people.

47. What are the sacraments?

The sacraments disclose and proclaim what God has done for the world in Jesus Christ, and convey its benefits to the community of believers. They are also signs of our allegiance to God. Protestant Churches recognise two sacraments: Baptism and the Lord's Supper.

48. What is Baptism?

Baptism looks forward to a life to be lived. It proclaims the grace the Father has shown in Christ to us in our helplessness, the forgiveness and cleansing of sin, the end of the old life of sin in the death of Christ, and rebirth through the Holy Spirit to new life in Christ. Baptism places us within the people of God and claims for us God's promised salvation and a share in the priestly calling of his children. From our side Baptism requires a response of repentance and faith in Christ as Lord and Saviour. Baptism is performed by immersing or dipping the candidate in water, or by sprinkling the candidate with water, in the name of the Father and of the Son and of the Holy Spirit. Baptism may be administered to an infant, in anticipation of a response to be made later, or to a young person or an adult in recognition of a response already made to the grace of God.

49. What is the Lord's Supper?

In the Lord's Supper Jesus Christ is present with his worshipping people and gives himself to them as their Lord and Saviour. As they eat the bread and drink the wine, through the power of the Holy Spirit they receive him by faith and with thanksgiving. They give thanks with the whole Church for Christ's sacrifice of himself once and for all on the cross. The Lord's Supper recalls Christ's Last Supper with the disciples. It proclaims Christ's passion, death and resurrection, unites the participants with him so that they are a living sacrifice in him, and gives them a foretaste of his heavenly banquet.

46. 2 Chronicles 5:11-14   Revelation 4; 15:3-4
    Psalms 134, 136, 138, 150
    1 Peter 2:9-10   Romans 12:1-2

Note: Worship may include silence, drama, music, dance and various art forms.

47. Matthew 28:19   1 Corinthians 11:23-25

Note: The Latin word *sacramentum* meant a soldier's oath of allegiance, and also a sacred rite.

48. John 3:5-8   Romans 6:1-14
    Colossians 2:2
    Acts 2:38-39; 10: 44-48; 8:36-38
    Matthew 28:19-20

Note: In traditions like our own which practise infant Baptism, the opportunity of public response is offered in the rite of Confirmation.

49. Mark 14:22-26   1 Corinthians 10:16; 11:23-29

Note: Some Christians call the Lord's Supper 'The Eucharist', from the Greek verb, *eucharisto,* 'I give thanks.' It is also called Holy Communion, because we all share together in Christ; and, by some, The Mass (from the Latin, 'I send'), because at the end we are sent out to serve Christ in the world in the power of the Holy Spirit.

50. Why are there many Churches?

The Church on earth is a human social institution. It therefore shares with all such groups the need to achieve its identity, to protect itself against threats, and to obtain and control power. From New Testament time onwards this has led to conflict, separation and hostility. Old historical divisions, however, are now weakening, and the twentieth century saw the rise, under the guidance of the Holy Spirit, of ecumenical bodies, such as the World Council of Churches, in which the different Churches can work together.

(e) Further study

Methodist Worship Book, pages 60-61, 114-115, 297-298

(f) THE FAITH OF THE CHURCH

51. Where can we find what Christians believe?

Christian beliefs are to be found in the Bible and, summarised, in the historic creeds (statements of belief) of the Church.

52. What is the Bible?

The Bible, comprising the Old and New Testaments, is the collection of books, gradually compiled, in which it is recorded how God has acted among, and spoken to and through, his people. The writers expressed themselves according to their own language, culture and point in history and in their different ways were all bearing witness to their faith in God. The Bible is the record of God's self-revelation, supremely in Jesus Christ, and is a means through which he still reveals himself, by the Holy Spirit.

50. Methodism: see Section (g)

1 Corinthians 1:10-17

Notes: Disagreements between East and West began as early as the 5th century. The *Great Schism* (separation) between Eastern and Western Churches came in 1054.

The separation in the West between the Roman Catholic Church and Protestant Churches of the Reformation came in the sixteenth century.

Divisions between Nonconformist denominations have continued since the seventeenth century.

Traditional Protestant emphases have been: the supreme authority of Scripture, salvation by grace through faith, and the priesthood of all believers.

(e) Worship
    Reading: Acts 20:25-38
    Hymn: *Singing the Faith* 675
    Prayer: *Methodist Worship Book*, page 539,
                  first prayer

51. Bible: see 52   Inspiration by the Holy Spirit: see 62

2 Timothy 3:14-17

Deed of Union, clause 4

52. Jeremiah 1:1-3   Hebrew 1:1   2 Peter 1:21

Note: We, too, when we try to talk about God, are frequently limited by the inadequacy of human language. See Isaiah 55:8-9

Deed of Union, clause 4

53. What are the historic creeds?
The Church uses two creeds which date back to the early centuries of its history: the Apostles' Creed, from the Western Church, and the Nicene Creed, from the Eastern Church.

54. What is the Apostles' Creed?
I believe in God, the Father almighty,
creator of heaven and earth.

I believe in Jesus Christ,
God's only Son, our Lord,
who was conceived by the Holy Spirit,
born of the Virgin Mary,
suffered under Pontius Pilate,
was crucified, died, and was buried;
he descended to the dead.
On the third day he rose again,
he ascended into heaven,
he is seated at the right hand of the Father,
and he will come to judge the living and the dead.
I believe in the Holy Spirit,
the holy catholic Church,
the communion of saints,
the forgiveness of sins,
the resurrection of the body,
and the life everlasting. *Amen.*

53. Note: The Western Church (Anglicans, Roman
    Catholics and Protestants) has also used the so-called
    Athanasian Creed or *Quicunque Vult*.   It was
    composed probably in the late fourth or early fifth
    century, that is, after the time of Athanasius (ca. AD
    296-373). It is in form more a sermon or instructional
    hymn than a creed, expounding the doctrine of the
    Trinity and opposing contemporary heresies.

    Trinity: see 65

54. The Apostles' Creed is so called because it
    summarises the teaching of the apostles of Jesus, and
    was at one time believed to date back to them. It has
    been used in the Western Church since the early days
    in the teaching of those being prepared for admission
    to the Church. It is used in the services in Section 3 of
    the *Methodist Worship Book*, 'Entry into the Church'.

55. **What is the Nicene Creed?**
We believe in one God,
the Father, the Almighty,
maker of heaven and earth,
of all that is, seen and unseen.

We believe in one Lord, Jesus Christ,
the only Son of God,
eternally begotten of the Father,
God from God, Light from Light,
true God from true God,
begotten, not made,
of one Being with the Father;
through him all things were made.
For us and for our salvation
he came down from heaven,
was incarnate of the Holy Spirit and the Virgin Mary
and became truly human.
For our sake he was crucified under Pontius Pilate;
he suffered death and was buried.
On the third day he rose again
in accordance with the Scriptures;
he ascended into heaven
and is seated at the right hand of the Father.
He will come again in glory to judge the living and the
    dead,
and his kingdom will have no end.

We believe in the Holy Spirit, the Lord, the giver of
    life,
who proceeds from the Father and the Son,
who with the Father and the Son is worshipped and
    glorified,
who has spoken through the prophets.
We believe in one holy catholic and apostolic Church.
We acknowledge one Baptism for the forgiveness of
    sins.
We look for the resurrection of the dead,
and the life of the world to come. *Amen.*

56. **What do we mean by belief in God?**
We believe that God, Father, Son and Holy Spirit,
truly exists as one God. To believe *in* him, however,
implies more than assent of the mind. Fully to believe
in him is to trust him alone for everything we need in
this life and for ever.

55. The Creed of Nicea was formulated at the Council of Nicea in AD 325. What we now call the Nicene Creed was formulated in AD 381 at the Council of Constantinople and authorised at the Council of Chalcedon in AD 451. This is the Creed used in some Communion Services in the *Methodist Worship Book*, and in Communion Services of other Churches.

56. Faith: see 12

Deuteronomy 6:4 (which can also be translated 'The Lord our God, the Lord is one.')
John 17:20-23   James 2:18-19

57. **What do the Creeds teach about God the Father?**
That he is one, that he is the Father of the Son, that he created all visible and invisible realms, and his immediate presence we call heaven.

58. **What do the Creeds teach about Jesus Christ?**
Jesus Christ is God the Son, who from eternity was with God the Father, sharing his nature, and acted with him in creation. Jesus Christ is God the Son who was born among us as a human being; in him alone we can see God the Father. Jesus Christ alone is both completely human and completely divine.

59. **What do the Creeds teach about Jesus Christ's coming?**
That in Jesus Christ God took human flesh and blood, and shared our human experience of birth, life and death. That Jesus Christ was not born of a human father, but by the direct intervention of the Holy Spirit.

60. **What do the Creeds teach about the meaning of Jesus Christ's life?**
He came to save the human race. He did this by entering into the human experience of life and death. By rising from the dead he demonstrated that there is no realm which is beyond the reach of his saving power. The resurrection also proclaims that Jesus has defeated sin and death. The ascension proclaims that Jesus Christ's work on earth is now complete, that he has returned to God the Father and reigns with him.

57. Genesis 1, 2   John 1:1-10
Colossians 1:14-17; 2:12-15
Psalm 73   1 Corinthians 15:24-28

Although we refer to God as almighty, because he has the power to carry out anything that he plans to do, he had shown through the cross that he does not use his power to prevent evil happening or to force us to do his will; yet he is able to transform evil into good and will ultimately triumph over evil.

58. Isaiah 9:1-7; 11:1-9   Psalm 2 (compare Acts 4:23-30)
Acts 2:22-36   1 John 2:22-23   John 1:1-14
Colossians 1:15-20   John 20:28   Matthew 28:18
Philippians 2:5-11   Romans 1:1-7

Note: Jesus Christ is called Lord because we recognise in him the full authority and majesty of God the Father, which have been confirmed by his being raised from death to share God's rule over the world.

59. John 1:1-14   1 John 4:1-3   Galatians 4:4-5
Matthew 1:18-25   Luke 1:26-56; 2:1-20

Note: Jesus Christ's unique birth was to be a sign that he came from the Father, and that his coming marked a new beginning for the human race.

60. The work of Christ: see Section (b) and accompanying references.

1 Corinthians 15:1-57   1 Peter 3:18-19; 4:6
Romans 8:18-23   Ephesians 1:6-10
Colossians 1:20
Luke 24:50-53   Acts 1:6-11
Philippians 2:5-11

Notes: The reference to Pontius Pilate, Roman Procurator (or Governor) of Judea (about AD 26-36) locates Jesus in history.

The evidence for the resurrection is the record, in the New Testament, of the testimony of those who were eye-witnesses of the resurrection; the testimony of those who have experienced him as a living presence throughout the history of the Church; and our own experience of his presence.

Jesus Christ's work on earth is now continued by the Holy Spirit through the Church. Acts 1:8
See: 1, 2, 3

61. **What do the Creeds teach about the second coming of Jesus and the final judgement?**
In his own way and in his own time God will finally judge the human race through Christ, bring all things together under the authority of Christ, and establish his reign of love for ever.

62. **What do the Creeds teach about the Holy Spirit?**
From eternity he is God. He has been present and active in the world from the beginning – in creation, in the inspiring of the prophets, in the equipping of God's servants.

63. **What do the Creeds teach about the Church?**
The Church is holy, because it belongs to God, who has set it apart to do his work, and because he is present in it. It is catholic, that is, universal, because through it God offers the complete good news about Jesus to every person everywhere, without distinction. It is apostolic, because it proclaims the same message about Jesus that the apostles did. There is an unbreakable bond, the communion of saints, between all God's people, in heaven and on earth, who rejoice together in all God's blessings.

The Church baptizes as a sign of God's free offer of forgiveness.

64. **What do the Creeds teach about the Christian hope?**
Those who trust in Christ receive now a foretaste of the new life in which they will share in Christ's triumph over death and rise, transformed like him, to perfect life in the presence of God.

61. Mark 13:24-27   Matthew 25:31-46

Note: Jesus specifically warned against speculating about the time of his return.

Acts 1:7   Mark 13:32-37

62. Genesis 1:1-2   Isaiah 61:1
Luke 1:35; 3:21-22; 4:1, 14
Acts 2:1-21   1 Corinthians 12, 14

Notes: In the New Testament (eg John 15:26) he is sometimes referred to by the Greek word *parakletos*, variously translated as Helper, Comforter, Advocate or Paraclete. The word indicates his role as the one called alongside to help and strengthen us.

The Holy Spirit was present with Jesus from his conception and throughout his ministry. He has been given to the Church to enable it to continue the ministry of Jesus Christ.

63. The Church: see Section (e)

1 Peter 2:9   1 Corinthians 14:24-25;
                                15:1-3

Matthew 28:19-20   Galatians 1:6-9; 3:28
Revelation 7:9-17

Baptism: see 48   Forgiveness: see 7, 8

1 John 1:5-2:2

Note: If Baptism is the sign of God's once and for all offer of forgiveness in Jesus Christ, the Lord's Supper is the sign of his continually renewed offer of forgiveness, to match our continuing need.

64. 1 Corinthians 15:35-50

65. What do we mean by the Holy Trinity?

When we think about the universe, and our place in it, and all that we have been given, we worship God as Creator and Father. When we look at Jesus, we see in him the expression in human form of all the qualities of God, especially love, and we worship Jesus as God and Saviour. Although Jesus has ascended to the Father, Christians have continued to experience the presence, power and love of Jesus in the Church and in their own lives through the Holy Spirit, whom we therefore also worship as God. Though we experience and respond to God in these three ways, we are not conscious of any division in God. The Bible rather suggests that Father, Son and Holy Spirit exist as a perfect communion. Therefore we worship one God, Father, Son and Holy Spirit, the Holy Trinity.

(f) Further study

John Wesley wrote of his hymn book of 1779: 'This book is, in effect, a little body of experimental and practical divinity.' Methodism has traditionally sung its theology. Compare the outline of Christian theology contained in the Contents pages of *Singing the Faith* with the outline we have been studying in this Section. Read the following hymns, and note how they illustrate the doctrines contained in the Creeds.

Singing the Faith: 1, 181, 199, 294, 335, 373, 688, 747, 764

(g) THE METHODIST CHURCH

66. How did the Methodist Church arise?

Following an experience in which he received an assurance of his own salvation, John Wesley felt called by God to an itinerant preaching ministry. With the support and help of other like-minded clergy and lay people, he preached in churches, in homes and in the open air, offering to his hearers the same salvation and assurance that he had experienced himself. Those who responded to his preaching he organised into religious societies, divided into classes, each with its own leader. He appointed helpers and assistants (later itinerant preachers and superintendents) to have oversight of the societies, which were grouped in circuits. The affairs of the societies were regulated by

(continues over)

65. Note: There are no specific references in the Bible to the Holy Trinity. But the doctrine is implied in all those passages which refer to Jesus or the Holy Spirit in the same terms as God the Father.

Trinity is a way of expressing briefly the idea that God is Three in One and One in Three.

(f) Worship
Reading: Acts 17:10-15
Hymn: *Singing the Faith* 157
Prayer: *Methodist Worship Book*, page 546, first prayer

66. Notes: The Revd John Wesley (1703-1791) was a clergyman of the Church of England. After a period of service in Savannah, Georgia, he returned to England, where his heart-warming experience took place, in Aldersgate Street, London, on 24 May, 1738. Among those who supported him the most notable were his brother Charles (see note below, 68) and the Revd George Whitefield (1714-1770).

The first Conference was held in 1744.

The Deed of Union (1932) states (Clause 4): "The Methodist Church ... ever remembers that in the Providence of God Methodism was raised up to spread Scriptural Holiness through the land by the proclamation of the Evangelical Faith and declares its unfaltering resolve to be true to its divinely appointed mission."

(continues over)

66. *(continued)*

an annual Conference of preachers. Although it was not John Wesley's intention that Methodism should separate from the Church of England, by the time of his death it had become a distinct Church.

67. What does Methodism hold in common with other Churches?

The Methodist Church is part of the universal Church. Its doctrines are based on the revelation of God in the Bible. It has received and preaches the gospel the apostles preached. It accepts the Creeds of the early Church. It accepts the principles of the Protestant Reformation.

68. What are the distinctive features of the Methodist Church?

Its message has been summarised as:

All need to be saved.
All may be saved.
All may know themselves saved.
All may be saved to the uttermost.

Traditional features of the Methodist Church include:

- the importance of lay leadership in preaching, pastoral care, and the administration of the local congregation;
- the importance of hymn-singing in worship and in the teaching of doctrine;
- the subdivision of congregations into small groups for instruction, pastoral care and fellowship;
- the circuit system, linking local congregations in an area, and the district, grouping a number of circuits;
- the Connexional system, linking all congregations through the annual Conference.

66. *(continued)*

In 1786 the Revd Thomas Coke, sent by Wesley to North America, landed in Antigua. This date is usually regarded as the start of Methodist overseas missions, but in fact many societies had already been established in America and other places by the witness of Methodist lay people.

The Methodist Episcopal Church in America was formally established in 1784 at the Christmas Conference in Baltimore.

67. The Creeds: see Section (f)
The Protestant Reformation: see 50 (note)

Deed of Union, clause 4

68. Notes: John Wesley's brother, the Revd Charles Wesley (1707-1788), wrote over 7,000 hymns.

The Conference is presided over by a President, who is elected annually. Each circuit is in the charge of a superintendent, and each district of a chair.

69. **Who are received as members of the Methodist Church?**
All those who confess Jesus Christ as Lord and Saviour and accept the obligation to serve him in the life of the Church and the world are welcome as members of the Methodist Church. If not already baptized those seeking membership will be baptized before being received as members, and those not already confirmed will be confirmed.

70. **What are the duties of a member of the Methodist Church?**
In the Church: A member is committed to worship, Holy Communion, fellowship and service, prayer and Bible study, and responsible giving.

In the world: A member is committed to the working out of their faith in daily life, the offering of personal service in the community, the Christian use of their resources, and the support of the Church in its total world mission.

(g) **Further study**
Methodist Worship Book, pages 281-296

69. Compare with 1, 2

Deed of Union, clause 8(a), (b), (c)

70. Duties of Membership: compare Sections (c), (d), (e)

Deed of Union, clause 9, as summarised on the ticket of membership, which is given to all Members, quarterly or annually. In addition to recognising membership, Methodism also maintains a community roll, which includes all members and adherents of the local congregation.

This Catechism is intended to provide a starting point for the fulfilment of the obligation to engage in prayer and Bible study.

(g) **Worship**

Read through prayerfully together the service of Confirmation and Reception into Membership (*Methodist Worship Book*, pages 97-102).

Are you now ready to respond to the questions in nos. 6 and 13 of the service?